seasons in bloom
SEASONS OF POETRY

dina ezzeddine

Seasons in Bloom. Copyright © 2023, 2024 by Dina Ezzeddine.

All rights reserved.

No portion of this book may be reproduced in any form without written permission from the publisher or author, except as permitted by Canada's copyright laws.

This publication is designed to provide accurate and authoritative information in regard to the subject matter covered. It is sold with the understanding that neither the author nor the publisher is engaged in rendering legal, investment, accounting or other professional services.

Cover Images used under License. Poem: Back cover poem created by Dina Ezzeddine and is subject to copyright.

Published by: Kindle Direct Publishing & IngramSpark, and all eBook platforms.
Cover design by: Cauldron Press Book Cover Design

ISBN: 978-1-0688396-6-5   (softcover)
ISBN: 978-1-0688396-7-2   (hardcover)

"Let the beauty of what you love
be what you do."

-RUMI

contents

SPRING

SUMMER

AUTUMN

WINTER

S P R I N G

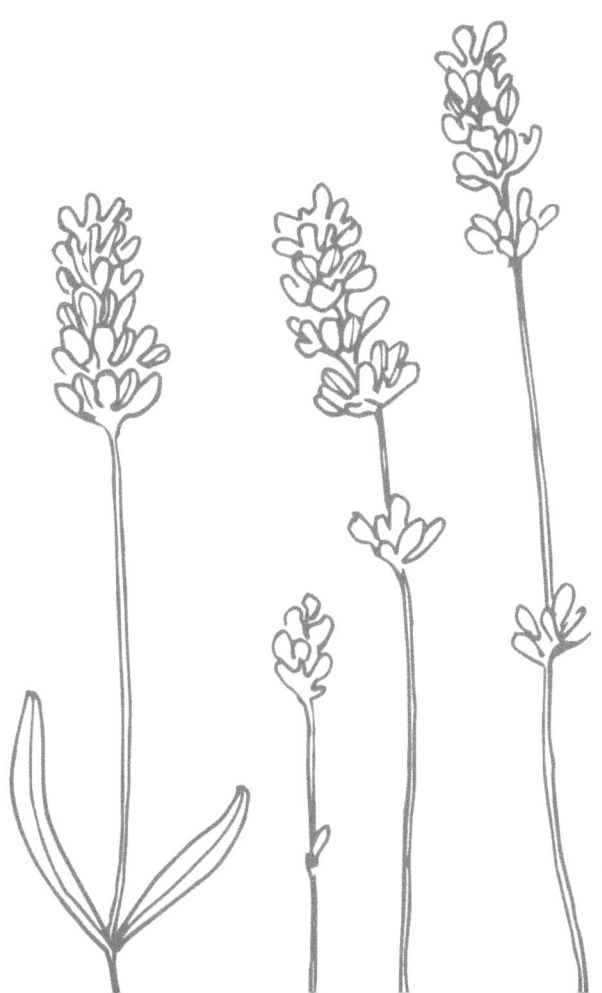

AWAKE... SPRING IS IN BLOOM

In spring, the world awakens from its slumber,
Blooms burst forth in a riot of color and light,
Nature's canvas painted with delicate brushstrokes,
Green buds unfurling in the warm sunlight.

Birds sing sweet melodies in the air,
Their songs a joyful symphony of cheer,
A chorus celebrating life's renewal,
As winter's grasp fades and spring draws near.

The earth comes alive with a vibrant energy,
A dance of rebirth and rejuvenation,
Each flower and leaf a testament,
To the beauty of nature's creation.

So let us revel in the season of bloom,
Embrace the magic of spring's gentle embrace,
And bask in the glory of new beginnings,
As we welcome the promise of love and grace.

ONE WITH NATURE... PHOTOGRAPHS

In fields of blossoms, photographers roam free,
Capturing the beauty of spring in all its glory.
Each bloom and bud, each color and hue,
Framed in their lens, a masterpiece anew.

The gentle breeze whispers through the trees,
As the photographers kneel upon their knees.
They focus, they adjust, they click away,
Preserving the season in a timeless display.

The sun dances on the petals with delight,
As the photographers chase the perfect light.
Their passion evident in each frame they seize,
A testament to nature's breathtaking tease.

With every shot, they capture a moment in time,
A fleeting beauty frozen in their rhyme.
Through their lens, we see spring's true form,
Immortalized forever, in their art so warm.

FLOWERS BLOOM WITH LOVE

In the garden, flowers bloom with love in spring,
Their petals dance in gentle breeze, so light.
Each bud unfurls, a symbol of new life,
With colors bright, a feast for eyes to see.

The air is filled with scents of fresh perfume,
As nature wakes from winter's frozen sleep.
The world is bathed in soft and golden light,
A time of hope and promise in the air.

The birds sing songs of joy and sweet delight,
Their melodies a symphony of peace.
The trees, adorned with leaves of emerald green,
Stand tall and strong, embracing life anew.

And in this season of rebirth and love,
We too can bloom and grow with hearts aglow.
For spring is here, a time to start anew,
To fill our lives with beauty, love, and truth.

SPRING GARDEN

In the spring garden, blooms awaken anew,
Each petal unfurls in the morning dew.
The daffodils dance with a joyful hue,
And tulips stretch towards the sky so blue.

The gentle breeze whispers through the trees,
As butterflies flit and birds chirp with ease.
The sun's warm rays kiss the earth with glee,
And fragrant blossoms scent the gentle breeze.

The garden thrives in vibrant colors bright,
As nature's beauty fills the day with light.
A peaceful haven, a tranquil sight,
In the spring garden, all is pure delight.

BUTTERFLY

In the light of spring, where flowers bloom,
A dazzling sight, a butterfly's plume.
With wings of grace, it dances free,
A symbol of beauty and harmony.

Oh, butterfly in spring so rare,
Your colors bright, beyond compare.
Each petal kissed by gentle breeze,
A masterpiece, like art to please.

Through meadows green, you gracefully glide,
In search of nectar, to satisfy your pride.
A creature delicate, yet strong,
Your journey in the breeze is long.

Amidst the world of new beginnings,
Your presence brings joy, a soulful singing.
A symbol of transformation and rebirth,
You remind us of the beauty of Earth.

Butterfly in spring, forever soar high,
In your presence, we find peace and sigh.
A majestic being, so divine,
In the tapestry of nature, you shine.

SPRING BIRDS

In spring, birds sing their sweet melodies,
Their songs fill the air with joyful tunes.
Each note a gift, each melody a gift,
As nature wakes from its long winter sleep.

Their voices ring out in perfect harmony,
A chorus of life in celebration.
Their colors bright, their feathers gleaming,
As they flit and flutter in the trees.

With each trill and chirp, they bring a sense of hope,
A reminder of the beauty that surrounds us.
Their songs remind us of the cycle of life,
Of rebirth, renewal, and the promise of spring.

So let us listen to their songs with open hearts,
And be grateful for the gift of their music.
For in their songs, we find a connection,
To the earth, to each other, and to ourselves.

GRACE OF SPRING'S EMBRACE

In springtime's gentle embrace, nature thrives,
Awakening from winter's cold slumber,
Blossoms unfurl, painting the world with hues
Of pink, yellow, and green, a vibrant palette.
Birds sing a joyful melody, filling the air
With sweet music, a chorus of renewal.
The sun shines brighter, warming the earth
And hearts alike, with its golden rays.
Gentle rains cleanse the world, washing away
The dullness of winter, leaving behind
A fresh canvas, ready to be adorned
With life's delicate and intricate designs.
In spring, hope blooms like the flowers,
Rejuvenating souls, stirring new dreams,
And reminding us of the eternal cycle
Of growth, rebirth, and endless possibility.

SPRING FLOWERS

In the heart of spring, the flowers bloom,
Their colors vibrant, dispelling gloom.
Petals soft as a lover's touch,
Blossoms that we love so much.

From the daffodil to the cherry tree,
Each flower holds a symphony.
A chorus of beauty, a feast for the eyes,
A gift from nature, a sweet surprise.

Fields of tulips, a rainbow array,
In the meadows, they dance and play.
Their fragrance fills the warming air,
A scent so sweet, beyond compare.

In this season of rebirth and light,
The spring flowers bring us delight.
They remind us of life's endless grace,
And the beauty of this sacred place.

So let us cherish each blossom and bloom,
For in their presence, we find our truest room.
In the epic tale of spring's sweet hours,
Let us celebrate the magic of the spring flowers.

SUNFLOWERS

In fields of gold, so tall and bright,
The sunflowers dance in the morning light.
Their faces turned towards the sun,
A radiant sight for everyone.

With petals of yellow, so warm and serene,
They tower above the grass so green.
Standing proud in their golden attire,
Spreading joy with their fiery desire.

They bow and sway in the gentle breeze,
Whispering secrets among the trees.
Their beauty shines for all to see,
A symbol of hope and positivity.

Oh sunflowers, so full of grace,
You light up the world with your smiling face.
Forever cherished, forever adored,
In fields of gold, you are truly adored.

LIFE IS IN...

...full Bloom

be joyful
 be happy

be blissful
 love life!

LIFE IS IN FULL BLOOM

In the meadow, flowers dance in the light,
Colors burst forth, a breathtaking sight,
Life is in full bloom, when spring comes around,
Nature's symphony, a joyful sound.

The air is filled with a sweet perfume,
A gentle breeze, a soft morning gloom,
Birds sing melodies from tree to tree,
A chorus of voices, wild and free.

The sun shines bright, warming the earth,
Awakening from winter's slumbered berth,
Each bud and blossom, a promise of new,
A tapestry of beauty, fresh and true.

So let us revel in this season of birth,
And cherish the gifts Mother Nature unearth,
For life is in full bloom, when spring comes around,
A time of renewal, a treasure, profound.

BE JOYFUL... BE HAPPY

In the meadows, spring has bloomed
The sun shines brightly, chasing gloom
Be joyful, be happy, sing a tune
For spring has arrived, none too soon

The birds chirp sweetly in the air
Their melodies bring a sense of care
The trees sway gently, green and fair
Nature's beauty beyond compare

Let's dance in meadows, under the sky
With hearts full of joy, reaching high
The world is alive, don't be shy
Embrace the moment, don't let it pass by

So be joyful, be happy, feel the thrill
Let laughter and happiness fill
For spring is in bloom, such a sight to behold
Let's cherish the season, as it unfolds.

BE BLISSFUL... LOVE LIFE

In springtime's glow, all are alive,
With joy and love, our hearts thrive.
Nature wakes, the birds do call,
A season of bliss for one and all.

The flowers bloom in hues so bright,
The sun shines warm, a pure delight.
Life's renewal in every tree,
Brings hope and peace for you and me.

So let's embrace this time of cheer,
And hold each moment oh so dear.
For in the spring, we find our way,
To be blissful and love life each day.

THE FLOWER CHILD

In a field of vibrant blooms she roams,
The flower child, with heart that glows,
Hippie life, so free and wild,
Embracing nature like a child.

Her hair adorned with flowers bright,
She dances in the morning light,
With bare feet upon the earth,
She finds her joy, her true rebirth.

She walks in peace, with love to share,
Her spirit light, without a care,
She spreads her message far and wide,
Of unity and grace, worldwide.

Through fields of green and skies so blue,
The flower child, her soul anew,
She blooms like petals in the sun,
Her journey just begun.

So let us all take heed her call,
To live in harmony, one and all,
Embrace the beauty of this life,
Just like the flower child, so rife.

WITH GRACE WE DANCE

With grace we dance in springs embrace,
Beneath the gentle sun's warm face.
As flowers bloom and birds take flight,
We twirl and spin in pure delight.

The music plays, a dreamy tune,
Enchanting us beneath the moon.
Our hearts are light, our spirits soar,
In this enchanted forest floor.

We move as one, in perfect time,
Our spirits lifted, hearts entwined.
With every step, we feel alive,
In this moment, we truly thrive.

So let us dance, in springs embrace,
With joy and love, in perfect grace.
For in this moment, we are free,
To dance together, you and me.

RELEASE YOUR WORRIES AND FEARS

In the heart of springtime,
Where the flowers bloom bright,
Release your worries, your fears,
And embrace this pure delight.

The sun shines down upon you,
Its warmth a soothing balm,
Let go of all that holds you back,
And be free from harm.

The birds sing sweet melodies,
As they dance in the sky,
Let their joyous tunes
Lift your spirits high.

Forget the troubles of yesterday,
Let them fade away,
Embrace the new beginnings,
That come with every day.

So release your worries, your fears,
And let your soul take flight,
Embrace the life of spring,
And bask in its pure light.

THE HIPPIE LIFE

In the heart of the 60s, a movement began,
Of free spirits and peace, living off the land.
They wore tie-dye shirts and flowers in their hair,
The hippies were a sight, a breath of fresh air.

They traveled in groups, in old VW buses,
Spreading love and kindness, without any fusses.
They sang songs of protest, against war and hate,
Their message was simple, it was never too late.

They danced at Woodstock, under the starry sky,
Their souls filled with music, their hearts lifted high.
They believed in harmony, with nature and man,
The hippie life was simple, it was their grand plan.

Though the years have passed, their spirit lives on,
In the peace signs we see, in the lyrics of a song.
So let's raise a glass to those brave souls of yore,
The hippies who showed us, love is worth fighting for.

BEE'S OF SPRING

In fields of flowers, the buzzing bees
Have returned for spring, their joyful tease
With wings aflutter, they dance and sing
Oh, how glad the arrival of the bee's wing

They sip from blossoms, sweet nectar dear
Gathering pollen, without a fear
Their work essential, for nature's balance
A sight to behold, their joyful prance

Through meadows green, they roam and roam
In search of flowers, their honeycomb home
Their gentle hum, a calming sound
Their presence in spring, a joy profound

So let us cherish, the bee's return
For they are key, to lessons we learn
In harmony with nature, they shall bring
The beauty of spring, on their delicate wing.

THE RAIN DANCE

In the hills where the wild winds blow,
The ancient people dance to and fro,
They raise their hands to the darkened sky,
And call upon the rain to satisfy.

With feathered headdresses and painted faces,
They move with rhythm in sacred places,
Their feet pound the earth in harmony,
As they pray for a bountiful destiny.

The drums beat loud in the twilight hour,
As they channel the spirits with ancient power,
Their voices rise in a reverent song,
To beckon the rain to come along.

The clouds gather above in a darkened dance,
As the people sway in a trance,
The rain begins to fall in a gentle stream,
Fulfilling the promise of the sacred dream.

The land is nourished, the crops will grow,
Thanks to the rain that the people know,
For their native rain dance is a sacred art,
A connection to nature that warms the heart.

THE ENCHANTED FOREST

In the light of wonder, a garden lies,
Where magic blooms beneath the skies,
Where flowers dance and trees whisper,
And every corner holds a secret, a whisper.

The Enchanted Forest, so fair and bright,
A place of dreams on a moonlit night,
Where fairies flit and unicorns play,
And laughter echoes through the day.

In this wondrous place, time stands still,
And all who enter feel a thrill,
Of wonder, joy, and pure delight,
As the stars above twinkle so bright.

The Enchanted Forest, a place of peace,
Where troubles and worries cease,
And in its beauty, hearts are healed,
By the magic that is revealed.

So come, my friend, and take my hand,
Let us wander through this enchanted land,
Where dreams come true and love is found,
In the Enchanted Forest, so profound.

SWEET ESCAPE

In my humble little flower garden,
Where colors bloom and fragrances reign,
I find my solace and my haven,
A sweet escape from all my pain.

Each petal whispers a soft tale,
Of joys and sorrows, love and woe,
In this sanctuary, I prevail,
And let my worries gently go.

The roses blush with pure delight,
The lilies dance in the gentle breeze,
In this garden, my soul takes flight,
And finds a moment of sweet peace.

I tend to each flower with care,
Nurturing their delicate grace,
In their beauty, I find a rare,
Kind of solace I cannot replace.

So if you ever need a place,
To find respite from the world's cruel hand,
Come join me in my flowered space,
And let our hearts in love expand.

THE HUM OF SPRING

In the heart of springtime's bloom,
When flowers dance and bees hum,
Nature's melody fills the air,
A symphony beyond compare.

The hum of spring, so sweet and light,
Brings joy and warmth to day and night,
Whispers of new life abound,
In every sight and every sound.

The birds sing songs of love and cheer,
As buds burst forth, the season near,
Green leaves rustle in the breeze,
A tranquil, peaceful, gentle ease.

The hum of spring, a gentle tune,
Echoing beneath the shining moon,
A testament to life's rebirth,
A celebration of the earth.

So let us rejoice in spring's embrace,
And feel its hum, in every place,
For in its song, we find our way,
To hope and joy, each passing day.

TRANQUILITY OF LIFE

In the hush of dawn, lies a peaceful scene,
Where tranquility reigns and all is serene.
The world awakens, with a gentle sigh,
As nature's harmony paints the sky.

The birds sing sweetly in the morning light,
Their melodies dancing through the day and night.
The rustling leaves whisper tales of old,
Of stories untold, of secrets untold.

The river flows with a soothing sound,
Its tranquil waters gently bound.
Reflecting the beauty of the world around,
In its depths, a peace profound.

In the quiet of the meadow green,
Where wildflowers bloom, and trees lean,
There lies a sense of calm and ease,
A balm for the soul, a sweet release.

So let us embrace this tranquil life,
Away from chaos, away from strife.
In the arms of nature, we'll find our peace,
And let our worries and fears cease.

DRINK TO SPRING

In the springtime when flowers bloom,
And nature casts off winter's gloom,
I raise my glass to toast the day,
With a drink that leads my cares away.

The sun shines bright, the birds they sing,
As I sip on my favorite springtime thing,
A cool and refreshing, fruity blend,
That's sure to lift my spirits in the end.

I drink to new beginnings in the air,
To all the beauty that's everywhere,
To the joy of life that spring brings,
As nature wakes from winter's stings.

So here's to spring, with all its cheer,
With friends and laughter always near,
With drinks that warm both heart and soul,
As we embrace the season's whole.

So fill your glass and raise it high,
To the beauty of the springtime sky,
And let the drink flow freely on,
As we celebrate the season's dawn.

HUMMINGBIRDS SING FOR SPRING

In gardens green where flowers bloom,
The hummingbirds flit in morning's gloom,
Their wings a blur of vibrant hues,
As they sip nectar, their delicate muse.

They hum and sing for spring's embrace,
A joyful chorus in sacred space,
Their tiny bodies sleek and fast,
A fleeting vision that will not last.

Through sunlit days and moonlit nights,
They bring a touch of pure delight,
Their songs a melody of love,
Sent from the heavens above.

So let us enjoy these creatures rare,
Whose presence fills the morning air,
For in their beauty, we can find,
A peace that soothes the restless mind.

Hummingbirds hum and sing for spring,
A timeless dance they sweetly bring,
May their grace forever soar,
In the heart of nature's lore.

DAISIES

In a field so vast and wide,
Where the daisies do abide,
Their petals white as snow,
Dancing in the gentle flow.

With faces turned towards the sun,
Their beauty shines for everyone,
A symbol of purity and grace,
In this tranquil, peaceful place.

Each daisy tells a story,
Of love, hope, and glory,
Their presence brings a smile,
Even from the darkest mile.

So let us cherish these flowers,
For they hold magical powers,
To uplift and inspire,
With their beauty that never tires.

LIVE...
  to the fullest

love...
  yourself

learn...
  always

LIVE ... TO THE FULLEST

In the dawn of spring, the world awakes,
A time of renewal, a season of grace,
Where flowers bloom and birds sing,
And life begins its wondrous race.

Live to the fullest, embrace the day,
For time is fleeting, don't let it slip away,
Chase your dreams, reach for the stars,
Let your spirit soar, break free from the bars.

In this epic tale of life and love,
Let your heart guide you, like a dove,
Through valleys low and mountains high,
Live each moment, never say die.

For spring has begun, a new chapter unfolds,
With endless possibilities, stories untold,
So seize the day, with all your might,
And live to the fullest, in the eternal light.

LOVE YOURSELF

In nature's bloom, love yourself,
oh my heart!
Embrace the beauty, in every part.
Through forests deep and valleys wide,
Let self-love be your faithful guide.

No storm can shake, no wind can sway,
The love within you every day.
In meadows green and rivers clear,
Let self-love banish doubt and fear.

For in the epic tale of life,
Self-love conquers all, amidst the strife.
So cherish yourself, in nature's embrace,
And let your love shine, in every place.

In oceans vast and mountains tall,
Let self-love be your constant call.
For in the end, when all is said and done,
Love yourself, oh precious one.

LEARN ALWAYS

in our world of knowledge, we roam
To learn always, we set our tone
With books and teachers as our guides
We journey forth, with open minds

From day to night, we seek to know
The wonders of this world we sow
In classrooms bright with passion's flame
We strive for wisdom, not for fame

Through trials and errors, we gain skill
To conquer mountains, and valleys fill
The lessons learned, forever stay
As we grow wiser, day by day

So let us embrace the journey ahead
With courage and strength, we will be led
For in the pursuit of knowledge true
We find our purpose, clear and new

In learning always, we find our light
To guide us through the darkest night
For in knowledge, we find our way
To a brighter, better, tomorrow's day.

LAUGH ALWAYS

In the meadows green and wide,
Where laughter always does abide,
Spring has bloomed its colors bright,
Filling hearts with pure delight.

The daffodils and tulips sway,
As children run and play all day,
Their giggles echoing through the air,
A joyous sound beyond compare.

The sun shines down with gentle grace,
Warming every smiling face,
Birds chirp and sing in perfect tune,
Underneath the golden moon.

In this season of rebirth and cheer,
There's no room for doubt or fear,
For as long as laughter fills the room,
Spring's beauty will forever bloom.

So let us cherish every moment,
And let joy be our only component,
For in laughter we find true bliss,
In the springtime's sweet and gentle kiss.

RAYS OF LIFE

In a world filled with darkness, so much strife,
We must all strive to share the rays of light,
In times of trouble, in times of trouble and strife,
Let kindness and love guide us through the night.

Spread happiness, let it shine so bright,
Illuminate the hearts of those in despair,
With each small act of goodness, ignite,
A flame of hope, a flame of love to share.

Reach out a hand, show someone you care,
Let them know they're not alone in this fight,
Together we can conquer, we can dare,
To share the rays of light, make everything right.

So let your light shine, let it burn so bright,
In this world of darkness, be a guiding light,
Spread love and joy, banish the night,
And share the rays of light in your life.

LIFE IS FULL OF SPRING

Life is full of spring, so vibrant and bright,
With blossoms in bloom and the sun shining light,
The birds are a-singing, the bees buzzing by,
In this season of rebirth, oh how time flies.

The air is so sweet with the scent of new growth,
As the world awakens from winter's cold troth,
The trees stretch their branches to reach for the sky,
And the rivers flow freely as time passes by.

In this time of renewal, we're filled with such glee,
As we plant our seeds for the future to see,
For life is a cycle, a dance to behold,
As we watch the story of spring slowly unfold.

So let us embrace this season of cheer,
And hold onto the memories we hold dear,
For life is full of spring, a time to rejoice,
In the beauty of nature's sweet, melodic voice.

BIRDS OF SPRING FILL THE AIR

In the meadows of the springtime bright,
When all the world is filled with light,
The birds of spring begin to sing,
Their joyful tunes on the wing.

With feathers of the purest hue,
In skies of blue they soar and view,
The blossoms blooming in the trees,
Their melody carried on the breeze.

From dawn 'til dusk they fill the air,
Their sweet songs banish all despair,
They bring to us a sense of peace,
Their music makes our worries cease.

So let us pause and take delight,
In the birds of spring taking flight,
Their beauty and their grace they bring,
To fill our hearts with joyous spring.

LIFE CAN BE BEAUTIFUL

In life's grand scheme, we hold the key
To shape our fate, to set us free
A ballad of choices, joy or sorrow
It's up to us to face tomorrow

Life can be beautiful, a song of light
With colors vibrant, shining bright
The laughter of loved ones, sweet and true
Embracing all that it can do

But if our hearts are filled with pain
And storms of sadness pour like rain
We are the ones who hold the power
To rise above, in our darkest hour

It's up to you, to make the call
To lift yourself, to stand up tall
For life can be a wonderful ride
If you choose to see the beauty inside

So let your heart be light and free
And shape your world, how it should be
For in the end, it's all on you
To make your life a dream come true.

DON'T LET YOUR HEART FILL WITH SADNESS

If our world is full of troubles, full of sorrow and madness,
Don't let your heart fill with sadness.
Though the storm clouds gather and the winds blow strong,
Keep faith in your spirit, and you will carry on.

Let not the weight of the world weigh you down,
For in every smile, a new hope is found.
In the darkest of nights, look for the light,
And the shadows will fade, giving way to delight.

Through valleys of tears and mountains of fears,
Hold onto your courage, banish all sneers.
For the road may be long, and the journey tough,
But with perseverance and love, you'll have more than enough.

So don't let your heart fill with sadness,
For in the end, it will lead to madness.
Embrace the joy, let happiness reign,
And your spirit will soar, free from all pain.

SPRING FILLS OUR HEARTS

In spring, the flowers bloom so bright,
Their colors dance in morning light.
The birds sing sweetly in the trees,
Their melodies carried on gentle breeze.

Spring can fill our hearts with a calming light,
And take away all our sorrows in flight.
The world awakens from winter's deep sleep,
Promising new memories to keep.

The grass is green, the sky is blue,
Nature's beauty comes into view.
With each new day, a fresh start,
Glimmers of hope in every heart.

So let us embrace this season of rebirth,
Let go of pain and find mirth.
For spring can heal all that's been torn,
And bring peace to hearts forlorn.

GOLDEN GRACE

In the meadows, where the sun shines bright,
Spring flowers bloom, a wondrous sight,
Petals of color, in the gentle breeze,
Bringing smiles and joy, with such ease.

The daffodils dance, in golden grace,
Tulips stand tall, in their brilliant embrace,
Lilies whisper sweet scents in the air,
As roses bloom, beyond compare.

Nature's artistry, in full bloom,
A symphony of colors, the earth's perfume,
Each petal, a masterpiece, so divine,
A gift from the heavens, a treasure to find.

So we bask in the beauty, our hearts aglow,
In the presence of spring flowers that grow,
Giving us smiles and joy, in every hue,
A reminder of nature's love, so true.

PETAL'S DANCE IN THE BREEZE

In the fields where spring flowers bloom,
Bringing color to the world's gloom,
Petals dance in the gentle breeze,
Announcing the arrival of summer's tease.

Each bloom a vibrant hue,
A masterpiece crafted anew,
Nature's artwork on display,
Bringing joy to each passing day.

But as the flowers fade,
Summer's heat begins to invade,
Clouds gather in the sky above,
Preparing to shower the earth with love.

Raindrops fall like tears,
Bringing life to the land it sears,
Nourishing the soil below,
So that new seeds may grow.

And so the cycle continues,
As spring flowers bloom and summer showers ensue,
A reminder of nature's endless power,
In the ever-changing seasons hour by hour.

SUNSHINE PAINTS THE SKY

In the blooming season's prime, when flowers dance
And sunshine paints the world in hues so bright,
In meadows green where butterflies prance
And birdsong fills the air with pure delight.

In the heart of spring, where life's reborn
And dormant seeds awake from wintry sleep,
The earth is clothed in colors, every morn
A masterpiece of beauty, vast and deep.

The trees stretch out their branches to the sky
And whisper secrets to the gentle breeze,
The rivers flow with laughter, never dry
As nature hums a soothing melody.

In the heart of spring, where dreams take flight
And hope springs eternal in every heart,
A time of new beginnings, shining bright
With promise of a fresh and vibrant start.

So let us bask in spring's warm embrace
And drink in all its wonders, far and near,
For in the heart of spring, we find a place
Where love and joy and beauty all appear.

NATURE'S BEAUTY IS DIVINE

Spring comes first and birds sing graceful tunes,
Awakening the earth from its slumbering dunes.
The flowers bloom, the trees sway,
A symphony of colors in a grand display.

The sun shines bright, warming the land,
Nature's beauty spread like a divine hand.
The rivers flow, the clouds drift by,
In this season of rebirth, we can't help but sigh.

The gentle breeze whispers secrets untold,
As life unfolds in a story so bold.
The animals frolic, the grasses dance,
In this epic tale of nature's grand romance.

So let us rejoice in the coming of spring,
A time of renewal, a time to sing.
For in this season of hope and light,
We are reminded of nature's eternal flight.

END OF SPRING'S BEAUTY AND GRACE

As the end of spring draws near,
Summer's heat begins to appear,
The sun shines brighter in the sky,
Golden rays warming earth and I.

Fields of green turn to gold,
As the seasons start to unfold,
Nature's beauty on full display,
In the epic saga of each day.

Birds sing melodies in the trees,
A gentle breeze rustles the leaves,
The world is alive with vibrant hues,
Nature's symphony, a beautiful muse.

As spring fades into memory,
Summer awaits with its own story,
New adventures and memories to make,
In the warmth of the sun's embrace.

So let us embrace this change,
As the seasons rearrange,
For with each ending comes a new start,
And summer is around the corner, ready to impart.

SUMMER

IT'S SUMMER TIME

In summertime, the sun's warm embrace
Sets the stage for nature's grand race
Flowers bloom and birds take flight
In this season of pure delight

The trees sway in a gentle breeze
As the world is filled with ease
Children's laughter fills the air
As they run without a care

The days are long, the nights are clear
As we bask in summer's cheer
Picnics, swims, and games galore
This season, we all adore

From dawn to dusk, we revel in
The beauty that summer brings
For in this time, we find our joy
In nature's epic, endless ploy

So let us cherish, let us adore
The wonders of summer, evermore
For in its warmth and light we find
A season that is truly divine.

SUMMER'S REIGN

Under the blazing sun of summer's reign,
The earth awakens from its slumbered state,
Nature dances in the heat's fiery domain,
Life unfolds in a grand and vibrant rate.

In meadows lush, the flowers bloom with zeal,
Their vibrant colors painting the landscape,
Birds sing their songs with joyous appeal,
A symphony of life in every shape.

The trees stand tall, their leaves shimmering,
In the golden light of the summer's glow,
Swaying gently in the warm wind's whispering,
A testament to the season's vibrant show.

The rivers flow with a gentle grace,
Their waters sparkling in the sun's embrace,
Life teems within, a thriving place,
A sanctuary in this fiery space.

In summer's heat, nature comes alive,
A testament to the cycle of life,
In this epic tale, we find solace and strive,
In the beauty of summer's vibrant strife.

BEACH TIME

Upon the golden shores we stand,
The sun dips low on the horizon grand.
With laughter and joy, we embrace the sea,
Creating memories that will forever be.

Family time, a special bond so true,
A connection that will always renew.
Together we build castles in the sand,
And walk hand in hand along the strand.

The waves crash against the shore,
A symphony of nature's roar.
We bask in the warmth of the sun,
Grateful for moments with loved ones.

As the day draws to a close,
We gather together, our hearts full and aglow.
In the beauty of this beach time,
We cherish each other, our love in prime.

For in these moments, we find our treasure,
A family bond that is beyond measure.
So here we stand, united and free,
Forever grateful for beach time with family.

FAMILY TIME

In the golden days of summer, when the sun shines bright
We pack our bags and hit the road, oh what a delight
With family by our side, we journey far and wide
Creating memories to cherish, in our hearts they abide

Through lush green valleys and towering mountains
We explore the world, in our own little fountain
Laughter fills the air, as we sing and play
Together we are strong, come what may

In the still of the night, under the starlit sky
We gather around the campfire, spirits flying high
Stories are told, of adventures past
Of trials and triumphs, that will forever last

As we wander through this beautiful land
Hand in hand, we walk hand in hand
A bond unbreakable, through thick and thin
Family trips in summertime, a treasure within

So let us remember these moments dear
That bring us joy and banish fear
For in our travels, we find our true selves
And in our family, our hearts forever dwell.

BREATHE THE SUMMER AIR

Upon the golden fields of summer's glow,
Where sunbeams dance and gentle breezes blow,
I close my eyes and feel the warmth embrace,
As whispers of the past time gently trace.

Inhale the sweet perfume of blooming flowers,
And listen to the melody of passing hours,
The breath of life in every blade of grass,
The symphony of nature, as seasons pass.

I drink in deep the essence of the earth,
The cycle of rebirth, of death and birth,
The sun-kissed air that fills my lungs with power,
In summer's embrace, I find my finest hour.

So breathe in deep the summer's sweet embrace,
And let it fill your spirit with grace,
For in the breath of air so pure and fair,
We find the strength to rise above despair.

In every breeze, in every rustling tree,
I hear the call of destiny,
And as I breathe the summer air so clear,
I know that I have nothing left to fear.

RICHNESS OF SUMMER LIFE

In the golden light of summer's grace,
The warmth of the sun upon my face,
The richness of the season's vibes,
Awakens me and comes alive.

The skies are clear, the air is sweet,
The flowers bloom beneath my feet,
The birds sing songs of pure delight,
As day gives way to tranquil night.

Oh, how I revel in summer's bliss,
A world of wonder, not to miss,
The lush green trees, the gentle breeze,
A paradise that puts me at ease.

I bask in nature's beauty bright,
Embracing every day and night,
For in the richness of summer's glow,
I find my peace, my joy, my soul.

SUMMER ROMANCE

In the heat of summer, love doth bloom,
A romance so sweet, like a fragrant perfume.
Two hearts entwined, in a dance so divine,
Under the golden sun, their love doth shine.

On sandy shores, they steal a kiss,
In the warmth of the day, they find their bliss.
Hand in hand, they wander through fields,
Their love a bond that never yields.

Through meadows of wildflowers, they roam,
Their love like a poem, written in the foam.
In the twilight hours, they whisper sweet nothings,
Their love a symphony, played by the strings.

As the summer days fade into night,
Their love burns bright, a beacon of light.
A romance for the ages, a love so true,
In the land of summer, their hearts renew.

So let us raise a toast to summer romance,
A love so pure, a passionate dance.
May their love endure, through all time and space,
In the epic tale of their summer embrace.

SUMMER:SPEND IT WITH YOUR LOVE

In the heart of summer's golden glow,
With the man I love by my side,
We stroll through fields of vibrant wildflowers,
Hand in hand, our love cannot hide.

The sun shines brightly upon us,
As we dance beneath the clear blue sky,
Our laughter fills the air with joy,
As we watch the world go by.

Together we explore the beauty,
Of the season that we hold so dear,
Each moment spent in each other's arms,
Is a memory we will always hold near.

Our love for summer burns like a flame,
Bright and fierce, it never dies,
With the man I love, by my side,
I am forever in paradise.

DIVE INTO THE DEEP BLUE SEA

In the deep blue sea, our journey begins,
A quest for treasures and wisdom, we're determined to win.
Beneath the waves, where mysteries lie,
Legends of old, whispered by the tide.

Into the depths, we plunge with might,
Exploring the unknown, guided by moonlight.
Through coral reefs and shipwrecks we roam,
Seeking stories that have long been unknown.

Creatures of wonder, with scales and fins,
Guardians of the ocean, where life begins.
Whales and dolphins, majestic and free,
In this watery kingdom, where we long to be.

But beware of the dangers that lurk in the dark,
For the deep blue sea holds many a shark.
With teeth sharp as daggers, they patrol their domain,
A reminder that nature's power will always reign.

So dive with courage, and dive with grace,
Embrace the beauty of this underwater place.
For in the heart of the sea, where dreams come alive,
We find our true selves, in this epic dive.

SEA LIFE

Upon the vast and rolling sea
In the depths of the azure sea,
Where creatures roam so wild and free,
They glide through waters clear and deep,
A world where secrets safely keep.

The octopus with arms so long,
Dances with grace, a silent song,
The jellyfish with colors bright,
Illuminate the dark of night.

The dolphins play and leap with glee,
Their laughter echoes endlessly,
While sharks patrol with silent might,
Guarding their kingdom day and night.

An explorer dives into the blue,
A world of wonder, ever true,
With each new sighting, heart expands,
In awe of sea life, vast and grand.

So let us cherish, love and protect,
The sea and all that we detect,
For in its depths, a beauty lies,
An epic tale beneath the skies.

SKY DIVING IN THE SUMMER

Upon the summer sky we soar,
With courage in our hearts galore,
A dive from heavens high above,
We find our truest sense of love.

The rush of wind, the thrill so sweet,
Skydiving in the summer heat,
Our spirits lifted, souls replete,
This moment, life feels so complete.

SUMMER PICNICS

In the lush green parks we lay,
Savoring the warmth of summer day.
Picnic basket filled with treats,
Underneath the shady retreats.

Children laugh and play in glee,
While the birds sing in harmony.
The sun shining brightly above,
Fills our hearts with joy and love.

A perfect day, so serene,
In nature's beauty, we convene.
Summer picnics, oh so grand,
In these moments, we understand.

HIDDEN PATH IN THE FOREST

A hidden path in the forest lies,
Where summer sun beams in the skies.
Through ancient trees we journey on,
With nature's beauty to gaze upon.

Wisps of mist dance in the air,
As we walk without a care.
Birds sing their sweet melodies,
Guiding us through the ancient trees.

With each step, a story is told,
Of legends and tales of old.
We follow the path, filled with wonder,
Lost in the forest, our hearts asunder.

But as the day turns into night,
We find our way back to the light.
And though the forest may be vast,
In its beauty, we are steadfast.

For in this hidden path we've found,
A peace that knows no bound.
And as we leave, our hearts are light,
Knowing we'll return to this place of delight.

SUMMER NIGHT'S

In the summer night, under the starry sky,
Dancing with the one I love, feeling so alive.
Our footsteps in sync, our hearts beating as one,
In this magical moment, our worries are undone.

The music fills the air, the rhythm takes control,
As we twirl and spin, our spirits soaring like a soul.
With every touch, every gaze, our love grows strong,
In this dance of passion, we dance all night long.

The moon shines bright, illuminating our embrace,
In the warmth of the summer night, lost in each other's grace.
With every step we take, in this dance so sweet,
Our love shines brighter, with every move we meet.

So let's dance in the summer night, you and I,
In this epic tale of love, under the starry sky.

SUMMER MUSIC FILLS THE AIR

Underneath the summer sun's warm embrace,
The music fills the air with joy and grace.
With every note, we dance without a care,
With the one we love, a bond so rare.

In this moment, time stands still,
As we move together, with precision and skill.
The rhythm guides us, we're in perfect sync,
In this epic dance, our spirits interlink.

So let us savor this summer night,
With our hearts full of love, shining bright.
For in this music, we find our solace,
Dancing with the one who brings us balance.

ODE TO SUMMER

Behold, the sun's warm embrace
Fills the day with vibrant grace
Summer's touch, so pure and bright
Bringing life to every sight

Fields of gold and skies of blue
Nature's beauty shining through
Life awakens, full of cheer
In this season, oh so dear

A time of growth, of love and laughter
In summer's light, nothing is after
Embracing all that's good and true
In this ode to summer and life, anew

So let us bask in the sun's warm glow
And let our spirits freely flow
In this season of abundance and bliss
Let us cherish each moment, in summer's kiss.

BEACH FRIENDS

On shores of sand and waves so grand,
Two friends did meet, hand in hand.
Beneath the sun, they laughed and played,
Their bond unbreakable, never to fade.

With every tide that ebbs and flows,
Their friendship blooms and steadily grows.
In sandy castles, secrets were shared,
In salty air, dreams declared.

Through storms of life, they stood steadfast,
Together they weathered, until the last.
On beach of memories, they remain,
Friends forever, no sorrow or pain.

BOOK LIFE, LIVE LIFE

In the summer's warm embrace, I sit outside,
Reading in the calm, where peace resides.
Birds sing their melodies, a sweet serenade,
As I lose myself in the books I've made.

The words dance on the page, telling tales of old,
Of heroes and villains, of adventures bold.
My mind wanders free, lost in the story's grip,
Each page turned is a new journey's ship.

The sun shines down, warming my skin,
As I delve into worlds where I've never been.
The breeze whispers secrets, a gentle touch,
As I lose myself in the stories' clutch.

Each moment spent in this tranquil place,
Is a treasure trove of wisdom and grace.
Reading in the summer, under nature's spell,
Is a gift, a joy, a place where all is well.

LOVE SUMMER, LOVE LIFE,

In the golden rays of summer's light,
We bask in love, so pure and bright.
Each day a gift, each moment savored,
In this season where all is favored.

Life's journey, a winding road we tread,
With love as our guide, no fear or dread.
Together we walk, hand in hand,
United in heart, a bond so grand.

In each other's eyes, we see our reflection,
A love so deep, beyond all detection.
Through trials and triumphs, we will remain,
In love's embrace, our souls sustain.

Let us cherish each moment, each embrace,
For in love's presence, there is grace.
United as one, forevermore,
In love and life, we shall adore.

LIFE SECRETS

In whispers of wind and rustle of leaves,
I share my secrets with the ancient trees,
For in nature's embrace, I find solace and peace,
And in her wisdom, my troubles they cease.

The song of the birds, the dance of the bees,
Reveal the truths that only nature sees,
In her vast expanse, I find my release,
And in her beauty, my soul finds its ease.

The secrets of life, hidden in plain sight,
In the changing seasons, in the day and night,
I learn from the earth, I learn from the sky,
And in their teachings, I never say goodbye.

So I walk among the flowers, I swim in the streams,
I bask in the sunlight, I dream in my dreams,
For in nature's embrace, I am truly free,
To share my secrets, to just be me.

THE FLOWERS HAVE A SECRET

In nature flowers have a secret,
Whispered in their petals so sweet.
A story of beauty and grace,
Hidden in their delicate embrace.

Each bloom holds a tale untold,
Of love, of life, of mysteries old.
In their colors and scents so divine,
Lies a message, a sign.

So next time you wander through a field,
Remember the secret that flowers yield.
Listen closely, and you may just hear,
The whispers of nature, crystal clear.

SUMMER TREASURE

In the heat of summer's blaze,
A treasure lies in golden days,
Beneath the sun's eternal gaze,
Nature's splendor on full display.

The fields of green, the rivers wide,
Where joy and laughter do reside,
The summer treasure we abide,
In nature's beauty we confide.

The chirping birds, the buzzing bees,
Dancing in the summer breeze,
Among the flowers and the trees,
Our spirits soar, our hearts at ease.

In every moment, every hour,
We treasure nature's boundless power,
In summer's warmth, we find our tower,
To stand strong in life's grand bower.

So let us cherish, let us savor,
The summer's gifts, our hearts to favor,
For in its beauty we find flavor,
A treasure to hold dear forever.

FLOAT IN THE RIVER OF DREAMS

In the river of dreams, we embark on a journey,
Through realms of wonder and magic so divine,
Where dreams take flight on wings of pure fantasy,
And the waters of time flow with a soothing rhyme.

We float on the currents of our innermost desires,
Guided by the whispers of ancient sires,
Through valleys of mist and mountains of fire,
To uncover the secrets of our deepest desires.

In this vast and boundless sea of dreams,
We discover truths that were long unseen,
And unlock the mysteries of our souls,
As we strive to reach our ultimate goals.

So let us drift on the river of dreams,
And lose ourselves in its enchanting streams,
For in its waters, we find solace and peace,
And in its depths, our innermost fears release.

SWEET, SWEET ELIXIR OF SUMMER

On the golden fields of summer's embrace,
Where the sun's warm rays caress our face,
Sweet harmony fills the air around,
As nature's beauty knows no bound.

The flowers bloom in vibrant hues,
Their sweet fragrance a melody that strews,
The birds sing in perfect tune,
Their symphony echoing under the moon.

The rivers flow with gentle grace,
Their soothing whispers a calming embrace,
The trees sway in unison,
Their leaves rustling in a harmonious son.

In this season of warmth and light,
Our souls are lifted to new height,
The sweetness of summer fills our hearts,
As we revel in nature's exquisite art.

So let us bask in this divine symphony,
In sweet, sweet harmony for all to see,
For in the summer time, under the sun's glow,
We are united in beauty, in blissful flow.

GOLD OF SUMMER

In the golden glow of summer's light,
We bask in beauty pure and bright.
Nature's treasures all around,
A symphony of sights and sounds.

The flowers bloom in vibrant hues,
Their fragrant scent a sweet muse.
The sun's warm kiss upon our skin,
A gentle embrace, a soothing din.

The rivers flow with crystal clear,
Nature's own sweet lullaby to hear.
Birds sing songs of pure delight,
As day turns into night.

We revel in this summer's grace,
In this tranquil and serene place.
A time to rest, a time to play,
In summer's beauty, we shall stay.

THE SUNS GOLDEN RAYS

In the golden rays of the summer sun,
We bask in beauty, each and every one,
Nature's colors vivid, the sky so blue,
A world of splendor, for me and you.

The birds sing sweetly in the trees,
As gentle whispers float on the breeze,
The flowers bloom in vibrant hues,
A masterpiece painted by the muse.

The rivers flow with a gentle grace,
A tranquil scene, a peaceful space,
The mountains stand tall and proud,
Their majesty singing clear and loud.

We revel in the warmth of the day,
In summers' beauty, we find our way,
A time of joy, of peace, of light,
In nature's splendor, our spirits take flight.

SECRET ADMIRER

In the heat of summer's glow,
A secret admirer I do know,
Whispers of love in the air,
But their identity I cannot bare.

Leaves rustle in the breeze,
As I search for clues with ease,
In every corner and every bend,
I wonder who my secret admirer could send.

In the shadows of the sun,
I feel their presence, the chosen one,
But their face remains unknown,
A mystery that has yet to be shown.

My heart beats with anticipation,
As I wait for their revelation,
My summer secret admirer,
Whose love sets my heart on fire.

SUMMER PRINCE

Oh my summer love, divine and true,
Each moment spent with you is like a dream come due,
Your words like poetry, a melody in my heart,
My secret prince, never shall we part.

In your arms, I find solace and peace,
As we wander through the forests, our troubles release,
Oh my summer love, a tale so grand,
Together we conquer, hand in hand.

BEFORE SUMMER LEAVES

Before summer leaves,
Golden hues paint the trees.
Nature's epic show,
As autumn starts to glow.
Leaves of red and gold,
Whisper tales of old.
Before winter's chill arrives,
We savor nature's thriving lives.

SUMMER DON'T LEAVE US SOON

Oh summer, don't leave us so soon
Your beauty we wish to forever swoon
The sun shining bright, the skies so blue
We can't bear to say goodbye to you

The flowers in bloom, the birds in flight
Everything feels just so right
Picnics in the park, lazy days at the beach
Oh summer, your lessons we wish to teach

So please, stay a little longer
Let us bask in your warmth, your wonder
For in your presence, we find joy
Oh summer, our hearts you truly do employ.

SUMMER WANES

As summer wanes, the fun must cease,
For autumn comes with a gentle breeze.
No more days of endless sun,
The season of warmth is nearly done.

We'll miss the late nights and poolside laughter,
As we prepare for the days that come after.
But fear not, for autumn brings a new start,
With crisp air and leaves that part.

So let's bid farewell to summer's delights,
And welcome the change with open sights.
For as each season comes and goes,
We find beauty in what nature bestows.

FINAL DAYS OF SUMMER

As summer's final days draw near,
The warmth begins to disappear.
The sun sets on the golden shore,
And memories of days of yore.

The trees begin to shed their leaves,
A cool breeze whispers in the eaves.
The laughter fades, the days grow short,
As summer's reign comes to naught.

But fear not, for in the fall,
New adventures await us all.
The final days of summer wane,
But soon we'll embrace the change.

AUTUMN

AUTUMN'S BEAUTY

In the midst of autumn's embrace
Beautiful leaves have fallen with grace
Their colors of gold, red, and brown
Creating a picturesque gown

The trees stand tall and proud
Their branches adorned like a shroud
Whispering secrets in the breeze
As they sway with such ease

Nature's artist at work
Creating a masterpiece, not a quirk
The beauty of autumn so divine
A sight that truly shines

As we watch the leaves descend
We know that this season will soon end
But the memories will stay
Of the beauty of autumn's display.

AUTUMN

As summer's warmth begins to fade,
Autumn arrives in a grand parade.
Leaves change colors, red and gold,
A sight to behold, a story told.

Crisp air and harvest moon above,
Marking the start of nature's love.
Animals prepare for winter's chill,
Autumn's arrival, a seasonal thrill.

MY AUTUMN HEART

In autumn's golden light, my heart does soar,
Amongst the leaves that dance, upon the forest floor.
The birds sing sweetly in the crisp, cool air,
Their melodies echoing, without a care.

The trees stand tall, in hues of red and gold,
Their branches swaying, stories of old.
Nature's beauty, a sight to behold,
As I wander through the woods, feeling bold.

My heart is with the autumn leaves,
Their colors dazzling, like a dream come true.
In this season of wonder and grace,
I find peace and solace, in nature's embrace.

HIBERNATION

In the golden glow of autumn's hue,
The trees painted in red, orange, and blue,
Nature's beauty truly shines,
As the cool wind whispers through the pine.

But alas, as the days grow cold,
Nature's splendor starts to fold,
The hibernation of the land,
Means the end of autumn's grand stand.

As the leaves crunch beneath our feet,
And the air turns bitter sweet,
We bid farewell to the season so divine,
As winter's chill begins to intertwine.

But fear not, for autumn will return,
With its beauty and warmth to yearn,
Until then, we cherish the memories we hold,
Of the beauty of autumn's colors, bold.

THE ORANGE GLOW OF LIFE

In the golden hour of twilight's grace,
Within the orange glow of autumn's light,
The sun sets with a gentle embrace,
Painting the sky with colors so bright.

The trees are ablaze in fiery hues,
Their leaves aflutter with the fall's delight,
Whispering secrets to the evening muse,
In the soft fading of day to night.

As nature prepares for its slumber deep,
And the world is cloaked in a hazy shroud,
I stand in awe, in the silence I keep,
At the beauty of autumn so proud.

In the orange glow of the setting sun,
I find peace in the fading light,
And I know that when the day is done,
There is beauty in the coming night.

PUMPKIN SPICE LATE

In the golden glow of autumn's light,
The leaves are changing, crisp and bright,
A chill is in the air, a hint of frost,
As nature's beauty is not to be lost.

The trees, ablaze in red and gold,
Shed their leaves, a sight to behold,
The air is filled with a spicy scent,
As autumn prepares, with great intent.

Pumpkin spice lattes, warm and sweet,
A comforting drink for those we meet,
Cozy sweaters, scarves, and hats,
Autumn is here, where beauty is at.

So let us savor this special time,
As nature's colors begin to climb,
Embrace the season, with hearts so full,
For autumn's beauty is never dull.

ELIXIR OF LIFE: BREATHE

In the crisp air of autumn's grace,
Breathe in the life it brings,
Golden leaves dancing in the breeze,
A melody that nature sings.

The sun sets early, painting the sky,
With hues of orange and red,
The world transforms before our eyes,
A season that's pure magic spread.

Take a breath, feel the chill,
As the earth prepares to rest,
In the beauty of this golden hour,
We find peace at its best.

So let go of all your worries,
And embrace this wondrous time,
For in the breath of autumn's life,
We find solace in its rhyme.

AUTUMN: MEANS EARTH SHEDS HER BEAUTY

In autumn's grace, the earth sheds her leaves,
A stunning sight that my heart believes.
The trees dress in hues of red and gold,
A beauty so timeless, a story told.

The crisp air brings a sense of calm,
As we walk through the woods, hand in palm.
The leaves crunch beneath our feet,
A melody of nature, so sweet.

The sky painted in shades of pink and blue,
As the sun sets, bidding adieu.
Autumn's magic, a fleeting glance,
A season of beauty, a lover's dance.

So let us cherish this moment in time,
As the earth sheds her leaves, so divine.
For in autumn's grace, we find solace,
A reminder of life's ever-changing pace.

EARTH'S KALEIDOSCOPE OF COLORS

The Earth's kaleidoscope of colors is autumn,
A symphony of hues that leaves us in awe,
The trees paint the landscape with their fiery tones,
A masterpiece of nature, no flaw.

The reds and oranges dance in the wind,
As leaves fall gently to the ground,
The cool crisp air whispers of change,
A season of beauty all around.

The warmth of summer fades away,
As autumn's chill begins to creep,
But the beauty that lies in the changing leaves,
Is a promise that nature will keep.

So as we marvel at the colors of fall,
Let's remember the magic that's in store,
For each season brings its own kind of beauty,
And autumn's majesty we can't ignore.

RUN THROUGH THE LEAVES

Before the last leaf falls,
Autumn graces us with its beauty,
Cold air, and laughter with friends,
As we kick through piles of leaves.

The trees sway in the breeze,
Their colors a sight to behold,
Red, orange, and yellow,
A canvas of nature's gold.

The crunch under our feet,
The smell of earth and decay,
Reminds us of the season's end,
And the coming winter's play.

But for now, we revel in the beauty,
Of autumn's fleeting grace,
And cherish these moments,
Before they vanish without a trace.

So let us soak it all in,
The sights, the sounds, the smells,
For soon the leaves will all be gone,
And we'll bid autumn farewell.

PAINTING IN HUES

In autumn's grasp, the leaves they fall,
Painting the world in hues so tall,
A fiery dance against the sky,
As nature's beauty catches our eye.

With each step, a crunch below,
A symphony of colors in a gentle flow,
The trees they shed their golden dress,
Creating a sense of peace and calmness.

As sunlight filters through the boughs,
Casting shadows on the forest's vows,
We're reminded of the fleeting time,
And cherish these moments, so sublime.

So let us pause and take it in,
The beauty of autumn, where life begins,
For in these leaves, we find our truth,
A reminder that even in endings, there's youth.

NATURE'S CANVAS

In autumn's painting, leaves ablaze,
Bring beauty to each passing gaze.
Their colors deep, their dance so free,
A sight that fills the heart with glee.

The golden hues, the crimson red,
A symphony of nature spread.
They flutter down in gentle grace,
A reminder of time's steady pace.

Through wind and rain, they still endure,
A testament to life's allure.
So let us cherish every leaf,
For in their beauty lies belief.

AUTUMN'S BEAUTY AND CALM

In autumn's beauty and calm,
The leaves fall like gentle balm.
Golden hues paint the trees,
Whispering secrets in the breeze.

Nature's canvas of red and gold,
A sight to behold, a story untold.
The earth prepares for winter's rest,
In autumn's beauty, we are blessed.

As the sun sets in the sky,
We bid farewell with a sigh.
But in our hearts, we hold dear,
The memories of autumn's cheer.

GRAB A TEA & A BOOK

In the quiet of autumn's grace,
Grab a tea and a book to embrace.
Sit by the window, let the world slow,
And bask in the calm, let your worries go.

Leaves of gold dance in the breeze,
Whispering tales of ancient trees.
The sun sets in a blaze of light,
Painting the sky in hues so bright.

As the season's beauty unfolds,
Let your mind wander, let your soul be consoled.
Embrace the peace, let the moment bloom,
In the magic of autumn, find your sweet perfume.

BEFORE HYBERNATION

In autumn's embrace, leaves fall in a hue
Of reds and golds, a majestic view
Nature gives us a rainbow of life
A symphony of colors, free from strife

Before hibernation, trees shed their coat
A fleeting beauty, a bittersweet note
But in this season, we find our peace
Amidst the chaos, a sweet release

So let us cherish this time of year
And hold onto memories, forever dear
For in the colors of autumn's fall
We find beauty, in nature's call.

WHAT DO LITTLE CRITTERS DO?

In the crisp and golden days of fall,
The critters scurry, big and small,
The squirrels gather nuts galore,
While chipmunks dig in earth's store.

The animals prep for winter's chill,
Enjoying autumn's peaceful thrill,
They frolic in the leaves so bright,
Before the cold sets in at night.

I wonder what they think and see,
As they prepare for slumber's plea,
But for now, in this autumn air,
They dance and play without a care.

DOES AUTUMN BRING YOU PEACE?

In autumn's golden glow we find
A peace that soothes the restless mind
The breeze whispers through the trees
Heralding a season of ease

Leaves rustle, dance, then gently fall
Nature's beauty touches us all
Before the Earth lies still and sleeps
In autumn's joy, our soul it keeps

So let us cherish these fleeting days
Embrace the calm in nature's ways
For in the quiet of this season's grace
We find joy and peace in autumn's embrace.

BEFORE EARTH SLEEPS

In autumn's grasp, a peaceful hush,
As Earth prepares to rest and blush.
The colors fade, yet beauty gleams,
A time of joy before our dreams.

The leaves that fall, a gentle sigh,
Whispering tales of days gone by.
A season of tranquility,
Before the earth's serenity.

Embrace the change, the stillness near,
Let autumn's peace dispel all fear.
In nature's calm, find solace deep,
Before our Earth stands still and sleeps.

THANKSGIVING FEAST

In autumn we have Thanksgiving feasts,
With pumpkins, apples, and turkey beasts,
Families gather around the table,
Grateful for all that we are able.

Leaves of gold and red adorn the trees,
The cool crisp air it gently breathes,
Harvest season full of cheer,
A time to be grateful, a time to be near.

So let us feast and give thanks with glee,
For all the blessings we receive,
In autumn's embrace we find our peace,
A time for love and grateful release.

AUTUMN JOY

In the crisp autumn air we find delight,
Just take some time to pause and sight,
Step outside and feel the breeze,
Let joy and cheer put your mind at ease.

With friends around, a laugh or two,
The season brings a joyful view,
The colors fade and leaves fall near,
Embrace the beauty of autumn's cheer.

CRISP AIR, BEAUTIFUL SCENTS

In the crisp cold air of autumn's morn,
I gather my pumpkins without any scorn.
The beautiful smells of harvest surround,
As I ready my home, for fall I am bound.

Orange and round, with stems so proud,
My pumpkins stand tall, in a festive crowd.
Carving and decorating, a joyful bout,
In this season of plenty, I have no doubt.

So I revel in autumn, with a heart so true,
Embracing the beauty, in all that I do.
As the leaves fall gently, and the air turns cool,
I cherish this time, as nature's own jewel.

AUTUMN AND PUMPKINS

In autumn's grasp, the air is cool,
A time for pumpkins, spice, and rule.
Lattes warm our hands with delight,
As we gather 'round the fire at night.

The trees are painted in hues so grand,
A feast for the eyes across the land.
The harvest's bounty, a true delight,
Great food brings us joy 'til the end of night.

So let us relish in autumn's grace,
Embrace the season, let time erase.
For in this time of pumpkin's cheer,
We find a reason to be near.

AUTUMN PRINCE

In autumn's sweet embrace we find
A love that warms the heart and mind
With golden leaves and crisp, cool air
Our happiness, a love affair

We walk hand in hand, through fields of gold
Our love like a story centuries old
As the trees dance in the gentle breeze
We embrace the season with such ease

Our hearts full of joy, our souls entwined
In this season of love, our spirits aligned
So here we stand, my love, in autumn's grace
Embracing the warmth, the beauty of this place

Together we'll cherish each moment we share
In the beauty of autumn, with love beyond compare
For in this season, we find our bliss
In each other's arms, in a timeless kiss.

REJOICE ITS AUTUMN

My dear friends, come gather 'round,
In the season of fun and warmth we've found.
Autumn's colors ablaze in the trees,
A gentle whisper in the breeze.

Rejoice in the beauty that surrounds,
As leaves fall softly to the ground.
The scent of pumpkin spice fills the air,
As we dance without a care.

With bonfires blazing bright at night,
Under a sky full of stars so light.
Together we'll laugh and sing,
In the joy that this season brings.

So let's raise a toast to our dear friends,
In this season that never ends.
May our laughter echo through the trees,
As we embrace the autumn breeze.

BIRDS STILL SING THEIR SONGS

In autumn's gentle breeze they sing,
The birds upon the wing.
Their melodies ring clear and true,
A song for me and you.

The leaves may fall, the days grow short,
But still their songs transport
Us to a place of peace and light,
Where everything is right.

So listen close, and hear their tune,
In the golden afternoon.
For in autumn, birds still sing their songs,
Reminding us where we belong.

COMFORT FOOD

In autumn days when leaves fall down,
And chill fills up the air,
We turn to food of comfort,
To warm us everywhere.

The kitchen smells of cinnamon,
And apples freshly baked,
A feast of hearty dishes,
To soothe the hearts that ache.

Pumpkin pie and spicy soup,
And roasted chestnuts too,
These comforting delights,
Will surely get us through.

With every savory bite we take,
Our worries drift away,
For comfort food in autumn,
Brings warmth on every day.

APPLE PICKING

In autumn's golden light, we roam
Through orchards ripe with apples sweet
A bountiful harvest calls us home
To gather fruit, a joyful feat

With baskets in our hands we go
Among the trees, their branches low
The scent of apple fills the air
As we pluck them, oh so fair

The leaves around us gently fall
As we pick apples, one and all
Their colors bright, their taste divine
A symbol of this season fine

We fill our baskets to the brim
With nature's gift, a gift so prime
And as we leave, our hearts a hymn
For autumn's beauty, in its time

So let us cherish harvest days
And pick apples in autumn's blaze
For in this season, we can see
The wonders of life's mystery.

WINTER

WINTER HAS PEAKED

Winter has peaked, its beauty surreal,
Snow covered landscapes that make your heart feel,
A chill in the air, a frost in the night,
Stars shining bright, such a mesmerizing sight.

The trees are bare, their branches stark,
Yet there's a certain magic in the park,
Children laughing, sledding down the hill,
Creating memories that time can't kill.

Fires crackling, warming our souls,
Hot cocoa in hand, feeling whole,
Snuggling up by the fire's glow,
Watching the flakes gently blow.

The world is hushed, covered in white,
A blanket of peace, such a wondrous sight,
Winter has peaked, but its magic lives on,
In the hearts and spirits of those who have drawn,
Inspiration and joy from this season so dear,
With memories that linger, year after year.

A FROZEN WONDERLAND

In winter's icy grasp we find,
A frozen wonderland divine,
Trees adorned in glistening white,
A shimmering blanket of pure delight.

The air is crisp, the skies are clear,
The world transformed, a sight so dear,
Children laugh and play in the snow,
Their cheeks flushed with a rosy glow.

Oh winter, you are a magical time,
A season of wonder, so sublime,
A time for cozy fires and hot cocoa,
A time to cherish, a time to know.

So let us embrace this frosty season,
And revel in its frozen beauty with reason,
For winter is a gift from above,
A frozen wonderland we all can love.

WINTER BRINGS PEACE

In winter's grasp, the earth stands still,
A blanket of white covers every hill.
The trees are bare, their branches cold,
Yet beauty in simplicity, we behold.

The chill in the air, the frosty morn,
Nature's beauty, winter adorned.
The world sleeps, in peaceful rest,
Awaiting spring's gentle caress.

In the quiet of winter's embrace,
We find solace, in this tranquil space.
The earth stands still, in frozen time,
A ballad of winter, simple and sublime.

TIME FOR ICE SKATING

In winter's chill, the frozen ponds await,
The blades upon the ice, they grate and grate,
With laughter ringing through the frosty air,
In perfect rhythm, gliding without a care.

The sun sets low, casting a golden glow,
As skaters twirl and spin, putting on a show,
Their faces flushed with cold and pure delight,
Their hearts beating fast, in the fading light.

The trees are bare, their branches etched in white,
Against the backdrop of the winter's night,
And as the stars begin to twinkle bright,
The skaters continue, lost in their own flight.

So take your time, enjoy this winter's night,
For in this moment, everything feels right,
On the ice, we're free, our worries fly away,
In this timeless dance, we'll forever stay.

PUMPKINS, AND SPICE AND EVERYTHING NICE

In the winter frost, the pumpkins glow bright,
With cinnamon and nutmeg, oh what a delight!
Spice fills the air, warming our souls,
Everything nice, as winter unfolds.

The crackling fire, the cozy embrace,
Pumpkins and spice, a comforting grace.
In the cold winter night, we gather near,
Sharing laughter and love, without fear.

So let's embrace the season so nice,
With pumpkins and spice, our hearts entice.
For in this winter's chill, we find such glee,
In everything nice, for you and me.

WINTER TIME IS FAMILY TIME

In winter time when cold winds blow,
Families gather, faces all aglow,
Around the fire, with laughter and cheer,
Sharing stories of the past year.

The children play in the snow so white,
Building snowmen in the fading light,
While parents watch with joy and pride,
Their love for each other can't be denied.

Winter time is family time,
No matter the weather, come rain or shine,
Together we'll weather the storm,
For in each other, we'll stay warm.

WINTER IS TIME FOR CRISP SNOW

In winter's grip, the world is hushed,
As crisp snow falls, so pure and white.
The trees stand still, their branches brushed,
With diamonds gleaming in the light.

The ground is blanketed, a winter wonderland
The air is cold, the sky is clear
The scene before me, oh so grand
A moment frozen, so dear.

I breathe in deep, the frosty air
And feel the chill creeping in
Winter's beauty is beyond compare
A season of magic, pure and serene.

So let the snow fall, let it cover the land
Winter brings a beauty all its own
A time of peace, of wonder so grand
In this crisp snow, my heart finds home.

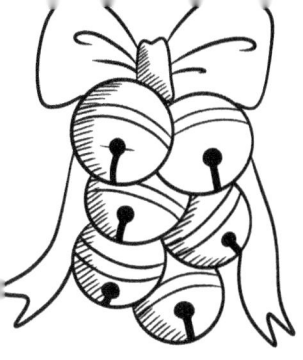

SPREAD HOLIDAY CHEER

In winter's chill, we gather near
To spread holiday cheer, without fear
With laughter, love, and joy aglow
Our spirits bright as winter snow

We deck the halls with boughs of holly
And share our hearts, so kind and jolly
With loved ones near and far, we're bound
In merry song and laughter's sound

So let us toast to days so dear
And spread holiday cheer, far and near
In this season of love and light
Let our hearts shine ever bright.

SKI TIME

As winter paints the world in a snowy hue,
Skiers gather, their passion anew.
With skis in hand and excitement in their eyes,
They journey to the mountains, where adventure lies.

Down the slopes, they glide with grace,
In this winter wonderland, they find their space.
The crisp chill in the air, the thrill of the ride,
Skiing time is their joy and pride.

With each turn and twist, they feel alive,
On these snowy peaks, they strive.
To conquer the hills, to feel the rush,
Skiing time, a thrill they'll always cherish.

So let's embrace the winter's call,
And hit the slopes, both big and small.
For in the snow, we find our prime,
A perfect day for skiing time.

WALKING IN A WINTER WONDERLAND

In a winter wonderland so bright,
The snow falls gently through the night.
I bundle up, my cheeks aglow,
Walking through the frost and snow.

The trees glisten, covered in white,
A magical and serene sight.
I crunch through fields of icy lace,
Captivated by the beauty of this place.

Each step I take, a soft sound hushed,
In this stillness, my worries are brushed.
I breathe in the crisp, cold air,
Feeling a sense of peace everywhere.

Walking in a winter wonderland,
I am filled with joy, my heart so grand.
Nature's beauty all around,
In this snowy paradise, I am bound.

WINTER IS PEACEFUL

Winter arrives with peaceful grace,
A quiet time, a quiet place.
The world is blanketed in white,
A peaceful hush, a calming sight.

The snowflakes fall, the earth's at rest,
Nature's beauty at its best.
The trees are bare, the sky is clear,
A sense of calm, a sense of cheer.

Icy winds may blow and bite,
But winter's peace feels just right.
A time to reflect, a time to dream,
Winter's peace, a soothing stream.

WINTER BRINGS SWEETS

In winter's chill, the sweets appear,
A warmth to banish cold and fear.
From gingerbread to spicy cake,
Our mouths with pleasure they do make.

The candy canes, the cocoa cups,
They fill our hearts with cozy love.
A taste of sugar, a hint of spice,
They bring a smile, they feel so nice.

So let us gather 'round the fire,
And satisfy our sweet desire.
For winter's treats are here to stay,
To brighten up our dreary day.

EGG NOG

In winter's cozy embrace, we gather 'round
To sip on egg nog, the sweetest sound
Creamy and rich, with a hint of spice
A taste of holiday, pure paradise

Whipped up with care, a cherished tradition
Bringing us cheer, a festive rendition
A toast to good health, and joy that abounds
In each creamy sip, love truly surrounds

So drink up, dear friends, and let us be merry
For egg nog brings warmth, even in the cold and dreary
A ballad of comfort, a drink that's divine
Egg nog, oh egg nog, forever be mine.

LET'S MAKE A GINGERBREAD MAN

In winter's chill, a tale began,
Of a Gingerbread Man so grand,
With a smile as sweet as sugar sand,
He ran and ran across the land.

His buttons were made of candy bright,
His laughter filled the silent night,
As he danced under the pale moonlight,
Oh, what a wondrous sight!

But beware the cunning fox's plan,
To catch the Gingerbread Man,
With a sly grin and a wicked hand,
He tried to capture him in the snow-covered land.

But the Gingerbread Man was too quick,
He dodged and darted, he made a quick flick,
And with a leap, he gave the fox a kick,
Escaping into the icy thick.

So if you see a Gingerbread Man,
With a ginger smile that you can't withstand,
Remember his tale in winter's span,
And keep him safe from the fox's hand.

MY SNOW SUIT

In my snow suit, I do delight,
As I frolic in the snow so white.
With boots that crunch and mittens tight,
I am ready for a winter fight.

The wind may howl, the snow may fall,
But in my suit, I stand so tall.
I'll build a snowman oh so grand,
And make snow angels in the land.

So here's to my snow suit, strong and true,
To keep me warm the whole day through.
I'll play and laugh, and then retreat,
Knowing my suit keeps out the sleet.

For in my snow suit, I am free,
To embrace the winter joy I see.
And when the day is finally done,
I'll cherish memories of fun.

ALL LIT UP

In winter, trees are lit up with light
Sparkling like stars in the cold, dark night
Their branches glisten with frosty delight
A magical sight, oh what a sight!

Snowflakes fall softly from the sky
Covering the ground in a blanket so white
The world transformed before our eyes
In winter's embrace, we take flight

With each step, we crunch through the snow
Leaving footprints behind as we go
The air is crisp, the wind does blow
But in this winter wonderland, our hearts do glow

So let us embrace this season so bright
Where trees are lit up with sparkle and light
In winter's beauty, we take flight
And find joy in the cold winter night.

CHRISTMAS WONDERLAND

In a Christmas wonderland so bright,
Where snowflakes dance on starlit night,
Families gather by the firelight,
To share in love and pure delight.

The tree aglow with tinsel and light,
Gifts wrapped up so neat and tight,
Children's laughter fills the night,
As they dream of Santa in flight.

Joy and peace abound this season,
Spreading love is the reason,
In this magical land of snow and pine,
The spirit of Christmas will always shine.

WINTER IS A CHEERY SEASON

In winter's grasp, the world is wrapped,
With snowflakes gently falling,
A time of joy, a time of cheer,
With loved ones close, hear them calling.

The trees are dressed in coats of white,
A sparkle in the sun,
The air is crisp, the sky is clear,
A day for everyone.

The fire burns, the cocoa warms,
As laughter fills the air,
Winter is a cheery season,
A time for love to share.

So gather 'round the cozy hearth,
And sing a merry tune,
For winter's magic all around,
Will surely chase away the gloom.

MY LOVE LET'S CELEBRATE WINTER

My love, let's celebrate winter together,
In the glow of the fire, through the frosty weather.
Let's dance in the snow, our hearts light as a feather,
As we cherish each moment, our love growing ever.

With snowflakes falling gently, in the moonlight's soft gleam,
We'll share sweet kisses, our love like a dream.
Hand in hand, we'll wander, as a perfect team,
Embracing the beauty of the winter's icy stream.

Let's cozy up by the fire, our souls intertwined,
As we sip hot cocoa, our love just divine.
In each other's arms, our hearts will find,
A warmth that lasts through winter, our love forever designed.

So my love, let's celebrate this season so grand,
In the embrace of winter, hand in hand.
Let's make memories together, in a winter wonderland,
For our love is a ballad, written in the snow-covered land.

NATURE'S BEAUTY IN WHITE FLAKES

Nature's beauty in white flakes,
Falling gently, no mistakes,
Blanketing earth in crystal lace,
Winter's wonder, nature's grace.

Each snowflake a work of art,
Crafted with a gentle heart,
Covering all in peaceful white,
Creating a tranquil sight.

Trees adorned in snowy dress,
A scene of pure loveliness,
Silent beauty all around,
Nature's canvas, so profound.

In this season of cold and chill,
Nature's beauty comforts still,
For in each flake that gently falls,
There's a beauty that enthralls.

TIME FOR UGLY SWEATERS

In winter's chill, we gather 'round
In ugly sweaters, we are found
A sight to see, with patterns bold
In colors bright, we won't be cold

We laugh and dance, without a care
In sweaters that we love to wear
Each one unique, a work of art
A cozy shield against the dark

So raise a glass, toast to the fun
In ugly sweaters, we are one
A time for joy, a time for cheer
In winter's warmth, we find it here.

TOUQUES AND MITS

In the winter's chill, when snowflakes fall,
We bundle up in touques and mitts so small.
Our fingers are warm, our heads are too,
Protected from the frosty morning dew.

With rosy cheeks and laughter bright,
We play in the snow from morning 'til night.
Building snowmen and having snowball fights,
Our touques and mitts keep us warm and tight.

So here's to winter, so cold and brisk,
With touques and mitts, we'll never risk
Getting frostbite or catching a cold,
As long as we have these, we'll never fold.

So let's embrace the winter cheer,
With touques and mitts, we'll never fear
The icy grip of the winter season,
For in our cozy gear, we have reason
To enjoy the snow and all its fun,
With touques and mitts, we are never outdone.

IT ISN'T WINTER WITHOUT TIM HORTON'S

In the depths of winter's chill so deep,
When frosty winds do blow,
There's a warmth that we all seek,
From Tim Hortons we know.

Their coffee strong and steaming hot,
Is like a cozy hug,
In a cup it hits the spot,
Oh how we all love.

From the first sip to the last drop,
It warms us to the core,
A comfort in a coffee shop,
We couldn't ask for more.

So in this season cold and white,
With Tim Hortons in our hand,
Winter feels just oh so right,
As we walk through snow-covered land.

THE COLD WINTER AIR

In the cold winter air, so crisp and clear,
Whispers of snowflakes, drawing near.
The chill bites deep into my bones,
As I walk through fields of ice and stones.

The trees stand bare, their branches white,
Against the backdrop of the fading light.
I pull my coat tighter, shivering with cold,
As the winter's grip, for me, takes hold.

But amidst the frost and the freezing breeze,
There's a beauty in the winter trees.
The sparkle of ice, the shimmer of snow,
In the cold winter air, my heart does glow.

So let the cold winds howl and bite,
I'll embrace the winter, with all my might.
For in the depths of the season's care,
There's magic to be found in the cold winter air.

DO YOU HEAR WHAT I HEAR?

In winter's chill, the wind does blow,
Whispering secrets soft and low.
Do you hear what I hear, my dear?
The snowflakes dance, the world's a-glow.

The trees stand tall, their branches bare,
Their silence fills the frosty air.
Do you hear what I hear, my love?
The echoes of the winter's stare.

The night is cold, the stars are bright,
A blanket of snow, pure and white.
Do you hear what I hear, my dear?
The beauty of the winter's sight.

So listen closely, don't you fear,
For winter's song is oh so near.
Do you hear what I hear, my love?
The magic of the winter's cheer.

REINDEER, ARE THEY COMING?

Reindeer, are they coming, so swift and so fleet?
With antlers so majestic, in winter's cold sleet
They dance through the snow, their hooves light as air
Bringing magic and wonder, for all to share

Their coats are so fluffy, white as the snow
Their eyes full of mischief, their smiles all aglow
They prance through the forest, under the moon's glow
Spreading joy and laughter, wherever they go

So keep a lookout, on a cold winter's night
For the reindeer may come, in a flash of pure light
With Santa close behind, in his sleigh all aglow
Bringing gifts and good cheer, to all down below

Reindeer, are they coming, with bells that jingle?
Bringing warmth and joy, in a winter so single
So let's welcome them in, with hearts full of glee
For the reindeer are coming, for you and for me.

SNOW IS GLISTENING

Snow is glistening in the land,
Covering all with a gentle hand.
Sparkling white in the morning light,
A beautiful winter sight.

Children play and laughter rings,
As they sled and slide in icy rings.
Snowflakes dance and twirl around,
Creating a magical winter sound.

Frosty trees stand tall and proud,
Their branches covered in a snowy shroud.
The world is peaceful, calm, and still,
As the snowfall blankets every hill.

So let us embrace this winter treat,
The snow, the cold, the frosty sleet.
For in the land where snow is glistening,
There is beauty and joy never missing.

LET'S SPEAD LOVE

In the heart of winter's chill
Let's spread love, kind and still
Through the snow and icy gust
In each other, let's trust

From the warmth of a fire's glow
To the shimmer of fresh fallen snow
Let's spread love, pure and true
In all that we say and do

In the midst of winter's cold
Let's embrace the love we hold
For in kindness, we find grace
And in love, we find our place

So let's spread love, far and wide
In this season, let it abide
For in unity and care
We find joy beyond compare

CHRISTMAS TREES

In the forest deep and green,
Stood a Christmas tree serene.
Tall and proud, covered in snow,
A sight to behold, all hearts aglow.

With twinkling lights and baubles bright,
It brings a festive, wondrous sight.
Oh Christmas tree, oh Christmas tree,
Fill our hearts with joy and glee.

As we gather 'round in love,
Singing songs from up above,
Our tree stands strong and true,
A symbol of hope and renewal.

So let us cherish this tree so grand,
A beacon of peace across the land.
For in its branches, we find cheer,
And the magic of Christmas, crystal clear.

MAKE A WISH

In the cold and frosty air,
When the snowflakes gently kiss,
Make a wish this winter fair,
And seal it with a whispered bliss.

Dream of sleigh rides through the snow,
Of cozy nights by the fire,
Let your wishes softly grow,
Fulfilling all your heart's desire.

The magic of the season's cheer,
Brings joy and love to all,
So close your eyes and hold dear,
Your wish, before the snowflakes fall.

Make a wish this winter night,
And watch as dreams come true,
For in the glow of moonlight,
All your wishes will pursue.

SNOWGLOBES

In winter's grasp, the snowglobes gleam,
A tranquil scene within the glass.
A world of wonder in a dream,
Where icy crystals gently pass.

Small figures dance amidst the snow,
A silent ballet frozen in time.
Their tiny steps so soft and slow,
In a winter wonderland so sublime.

The snowflakes fall in swirling grace,
A delicate blanket on the ground.
Each scene a tiny, frozen space,
A peaceful moment to be found.

So shake the globe and watch it snow,
A miniature world in your hand.
In winter's glow, a beauty to show,
In the snowglobes of this land.

DECK THE HALLS

Deck the halls with bells of holly,
Tis the season to be jolly.
Snowflakes falling, winter's call,
Festive spirits, one and all.

Gather 'round the crackling fire,
With loved ones near, hearts full of desire.
Sing of joy and peace on earth,
Celebrating Jesus' birth.

Christmas cheer fills the air,
Grateful for all that we share.
Hark the herald angels sing,
Praises to our heavenly king.

So deck the halls with bells of holly,
Spread good tidings, not melancholy.
For this season is a time of light,
Shining bright in winter's night.

JOY TO THE WORLD: AND ALL OF US

In winter's chill, the world is bright
With joy that fills the day and night
A time for laughter, love, and cheer
For all to hold their loved ones near

The snow it falls, a blanket white
That glistens in the soft moonlight
Each flake a shimmering, sparkling gem
A sign that peace will never end

Joy to the world and all of us
In winter's glow, we find our trust
In each other, in ourselves
In the love that in our hearts dwells

So let us sing and let us dance
In this season's sweet romance
For winter brings us all together
In joy that will last forever.

SOON WINTER WILL END

In the depths of winter's icy hold,
The world outside is bleak and cold,
But soon the frost will melt away,
And spring will come to save the day.

The days grow longer, the sun shines bright,
The birds return, taking to flight,
The flowers bloom, the grass turns green,
The world awakens from its icy dream.

So let us cherish this season's end,
As winter fades and spring begins,
For soon the snow will disappear,
And warmer days will soon be here.

SPREAD LOVE NOT HATE

In the winter's chill, let love be our guide,
Spread kindness and warmth, let hate subside.
Through valleys dark and mountains high,
Let love be the beacon that lights up the sky.

In a world so cold and full of strife,
Let's choose love over anger, bring hope to life.
With every word and every deed,
Let's sow seeds of love that others may heed.

For in this season of cold and frost,
Let's spread love, not hate, at any cost.
Let's build bridges, not walls of hate,
And make the world a kinder place.

So let's join hands, in love unite,
And banish darkness with love's light.
Let's be the change we wish to see,
And spread love, not hate, for all to be free.

IN THIS COLLECTION
GRAB YOUR COPY TODAY!

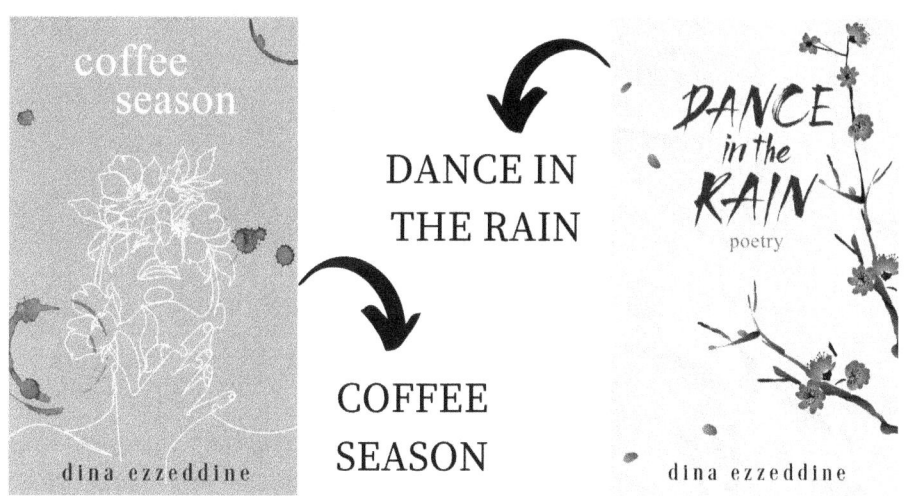

DANCE IN THE RAIN

COFFEE SEASON

THINGS I CAN'T SAY

SEASONS IN BLOOM

AMAZON, BARNES & NOBLE, COLES/INDIGO BOOK STORES & EVERYWHERE!

OTHER BOOKS BY THE AUTHOR

CHILDREN'S BOOKS

. Toshi and the missing Ball-y
. Toshi visits London, England
. Toshi visits Pairs, France
. Toshi in Tokyo
. Toshi and his human sisters

TOSHI AND THE MISSING BALL-Y

OUT NOW! GRAB YOUR COPY!

A Note on the Author

Dina Ezzeddine is a writer and illustrator from Canada. Dina has a degree in Visual Arts and Design, as well as a Bachelor of Arts degree in English. Dina has written numerous children's book and numerous teen books. This book of poetry is her latest work. You can find more of Dina's upcoming work online!

Find more of Dina's here:
visit Amazon & Barnes & Noble

- author_illustratordina
- aiko10195@gmail.com
- missDinaAuthor

LEAVE US A REVIEW!

☆☆☆☆☆

Give us your opinions and thoughts
on any of our works!
Wherever books are sold!

SAM COOPER HATES BULLIES

Samantha Cooper, a 10-year-old girl who refuses to be intimidated by the school bully, meets Tiffany Simmons. When Samantha begins a new school, Tiffany and her gang make her life miserable, but Samantha's determination to stand up for herself and others leads her to an unlikely ally. Sam meets Max, and Nate, two quiet school nerds, who has been bullied by Tiffany. Together, they devise a plan to expose Tiffany's true colors at the school's talent show. However, as they prepare for their big moment, they face unexpected challenges and learn the true meaning of courage, empathy and friendship. Will Sam, Max and Nate's bravery be enough to bring down the school bully and restore peace to the school? Dive into this inspiring tale of self-discovery and empowerment and find out.

PRE-ORDER YOUR COPY TODAY!!

Releasing October 25, 2024 on all platforms.

AMAZON, and Barnes & Noble and all e-book platforms.

www.ingramcontent.com/pod-product-compliance
Lightning Source LLC
Chambersburg PA
CBHW051600010526
44118CB00023B/2762